The Burgess Shale

Margaret Atwood

CLC Kreisel Lecture Series

The Burgess Shale

The Canadian Writing Landscape of the 1960s

The University of Alberta Press

Published by

The University of Alberta Press
Ring House 2
Edmonton, Alberta, Canada T6G 2E1
www.uap.ualberta.ca
and
Canadian Literature Centre /
Centre de littérature canadienne
3–5 Humanities Centre
University of Alberta
Edmonton, Alberta, Canada T6G 2E5
www.abclc.ca

LIBRARY AND ARCHIVES CANADA
CATALOGUING IN PUBLICATION

Atwood, Margaret, 1939–, author
The Burgess Shale : the Canadian writing landscape of the 1960s / Margaret Atwood.

(CLC Kreisel lecture series)
Issued in print and electronic formats.
Co-published by: Canadian Literature Centre.
ISBN 978-1-77212-301-2 (softcover).—
ISBN 978-1-77212-304-3 (EPUB).—
ISBN 978-1-77212-305-0 (Kindle).—
ISBN 978-1-77212-306-7 (PDF)

1. Canadian literature (English)—20th century—History and criticism. I. Canadian Literature Centre, issuing body II. Title. III. Series: Henry Kreisel lecture series

PS8071.4.A89 2017 C810.9'0054
C2016-908097-8 C2016-908098-6

First edition, first printing, 2017.
Printed and bound in Canada by Houghton Boston Printers, Saskatoon, Saskatchewan.
Copyediting and proofreading by Peter Midgley.

The University of Alberta Press is committed to protecting our natural environment. As part of our efforts, this book is printed on Enviro Paper: it contains 100% post-consumer recycled fibres and is acid- and chlorine-free.

The Canadian Literature Centre acknowledges the support of the Alberta Foundation for the Arts for the CLC Kreisel Lecture delivered by Margaret Atwood in April 2016 at the Winspear Centre.

The University of Alberta Press gratefully acknowledges the support received for its publishing program from the Government of Canada, the Canada Council for the Arts, and the Government of Alberta through the Alberta Media Fund.

Canada

Foreword / Liminaire

The CLC Kreisel Lecture Series / La collection des Conférences Kreisel du CLC

WHEN I ARRIVED at the University of Alberta in 2008, the CLC was just more than a fledgling year and a half. And now, I feel like the proud parent of a gifted ten-year-old. The Canadian Literature Centre is a unique space for bilingual and multicultural reading and research, bringing people together through critical, professional, intellectual, and social alliances. It is a place where readers come to listen, authors to read, students to learn, professors to teach, and researchers to share. All of us come to the CLC to celebrate the incredible writing in this country. From the Brown Bag Lunch reading series to the Annual Research Seminars, from the Scholarly Lecture series to the CLC Kreisel Lectures featured in these pages, the CLC is a public forum for inclusive thinking, challenging criticism, and varied forms of literary circulation and production. This past decade, the CLC has organized and co-organized eight international conferences, with six ensuing collections of essays, written in English and in French, either published or currently in press. With a critical anthology, *Ten Canadian Writers in Context*, commemorating ten years of the Brown Bag Lunch reading series and published in 2016, CLC staff and researchers have also completed a digital archive, *Inside the Bag: Can Lit Alive!* of live video recordings,

Proust Questionnaires, and exhaustive, searchable bibliographical content for open public access. This lecture by Margaret Atwood will be a culminating tenth title in the Kreisel series, and is co-published by the University of Alberta Press and the CLC. We are tremendously honoured and excited to welcome Canada's best-known literary *grande dame* to the stage to help us mark the CLC's tenth anniversary.

Les Conférences Kreisel du CLC abordent les grandes questions qui nous concernent tous et toutes dans la spécificité de notre vécu contemporain, peu importent nos différences. Dans une intention de dialogue libre et honnête, ces conférences reflètent l'ardeur et la profondeur intellectuelles ainsi que l'humour et l'élégance des dix auteurs extrêmement doués et présentés jusqu'ici : Joseph Boyden, Wayne Johnston, Dany Laferrière, Eden Robinson, Annabel Lyon, Lawrence Hill, Esi Edugyan, Tomson Highway, Lynn Coady, et désormais, Margaret Atwood. Pensons aux fines observations de Boyden sur l'oppression sociale, les identités culturelles et le lieu; ou à la réflexion de Johnston sur la rencontre tumultueuse de l'histoire et la fiction. Tenons compte avec Laferrière des épreuves de l'exil et des joies de la migrance; ou de l'éthique personnelle et communautaire du récit autochtone que nous présente Robinson. L'antiquité et le présent se réunissent dans la conférence de Lyon au sujet du mode créatif de la fiction historique. Hill plaide le besoin d'une conversation informée sur la censure des livres. Highway défend l'apprentissage libérateur et heureux *d'autres langues, de la langue des autres*, y compris le langage de la musique. Coady nous incite à analyser l'alarmisme culturel quant à l'avenir du livre à l'ère numérique. Et ici, Atwood nous présente un rappel pittoresque et nécessaire de notre histoire littéraire.

These public lectures also set out to honour Professor Henry Kreisel's legacy in an annual public forum. Author, University Professor and Officer of the Order of Canada, Henry Kreisel was born in Vienna into a Jewish family in 1922. He left his homeland for England in 1938 and was interned, in Canada, for eighteen months during the Second World War. After studying at the University of Toronto, he began teaching in 1947 at the University of Alberta, and served as Chair of English from 1961 until 1970. He served as Vice-President (Academic) from 1970 to 1975, and was named University Professor in 1975, the highest scholarly award bestowed on its faculty members by the University of Alberta. Professor Kreisel was an inspiring and beloved teacher who taught generations of students to love literature and was one of the first people to bring the experience of the immigrant to modern Canadian literature. He died in Edmonton in 1991. His works include two novels, *The Rich Man* (1948) and *The Betrayal* (1964), and a collection of short stories, *The Almost Meeting* (1981). His internment diary, alongside critical essays on his writing, appears in *Another Country: Writings By and About Henry Kreisel* (1985). The generosity of Professor Kreisel's teaching at the University of Alberta profoundly inspires the CLC in its public outreach, research pursuits, and continued commitment to the ever-growing richness and diversity of Canada's writings. The Centre embraces Henry Kreisel's no less than pioneering focus on the knowledge of one's own literatures. The CLC seeks and fosters a better understanding of a complicated and difficult world, which literature can reimagine and perhaps even transform.

To return to my parental metaphor, it takes a whole village to raise a child. So goes the Igbo and Yoruba proverb. The values of community, relationship, care, and hospitality contained in this Nigerian proverb could not better conjure the ways in which the CLC has grown into adulthood. With the continued generosity of CLC founder and benefactor Dr. Eric Schloss, the steadfast support from the Dean's Office in the Faculty of Arts at the University of Alberta, and donations from our friends who believe in our mission, the CLC simply would not exist. Ongoing programming with community partners, such as Edmonton's Poetry Festival and LitFest: Edmonton's Nonfiction Festival which marked its own tenth anniversary in 2016, has been paramount to the Centre's public outreach, which is indeed at the heart and soul of its research mandate.

Enfin, il nous semble particulièrement juste que la conférence de Margaret Atwood pose un regard en arrière sur l'histoire de la modernité littéraire au Canada, tout comme plusieurs d'entre nous affiliés d'une manière ou d'une autre au CLC posons un regard en arrière sur ces dix années de textes rédigés, récités, édités, analysés, discutés et aimés. C'est par amour de la littérature que nous nous rassemblons pour parler de littérature canadienne, grâce au soin de sa saine production et sa libre circulation dans nos réseaux collectifs et intimes. Bon anniversaire à nous tous!

MARIE CARRIÈRE
Director/Directrice
Canadian Literature Centre/Centre de littérature canadienne
Edmonton, November 2016

Introduction

EDMONTON'S ARTS MAGAZINE, *The Yards*, perhaps said it best in the weeks leading up to the 2016 CLC Kreisel Lecture: "Who better for the Canadian Literature Centre to invite for its 10th annual Kreisel Lecture than the country's best-known author?" Who better indeed? Margaret Atwood is not only Canada's best-known author, but also one of the most productive writers of her time. As a novelist, outspoken environmentalist, feminist, poet, librettist, critic, and satirist, she has cultivated an international reputation. As the following lecture demonstrates, Margaret Atwood is one of the very founders of what we consider "Canadian" literature to be today. She was instrumental in dreaming it up and making it happen.

Margaret Atwood's first collection of poetry, *Double Persephone*, appeared in 1961. This self-published book, hand-set and designed by the author herself, went on to win the E.J. Pratt Medal. The rest, as they say, is history. If the concern with doubleness and revival marked the early forays into poetry, Margaret Atwood's exploration of what she termed as Canada's "paranoid schizophrenia" in *The Journals of Susanna Moodie* also foreshadowed her interests in Canadian culture and historiography, which she would pursue throughout her writing career. "I am a word/in a foreign language," wrote Atwood's very own pioneering Mrs. Moodie in 1970, speaking from the haunted underground of settler-invader identity crisis and survival.

Women draw a huge figure in the historical as well as narrative landscapes of Atwoodian fiction—whether they are pulled back into the northern wilderness of their childhood as in the novel *Surfacing* (1972), or fighting on the battle ground of femininity and all of its trappings as in the novels *The Edible Woman* (1968), *Lady Oracle* (1976), *Cat's Eye* (1988), and *The Robber Bride* (1993). Unruly female heroines have since emerged to disrupt the nation and its colonial mindset, including the unforgettable Grace Marks of *Alias Grace* and Iris Chase Griffen of the Man Booker Prize–winning novel, *The Blind Assassin*. The gothic, macabre, or disorderly aspects of these women have not been lost on the veritable plethora of literary criticism written on Atwood's work. Nor has Margaret Atwood's own literary use of birds and animals gone unanalyzed. The hybrid, often female, human-animal forms—the insects, the vultures, the pigs with human cortexes, the "liolambs" with human hair, and soon the part-cat, part-bird superhero of a new graphic novel—occupy the post-human tapestry of her writing. But it was the poetry collection, *The Animals in that Country*, which was first to set Atwood's bestiary in motion: "In this country," wrote the poet back in 1967, "the animals / have the faces / of people."

To some extent, the repercussions of the 9/11 attacks have fuelled Margaret Atwood's post-millennial writing. The very real threats of bioterrorism, state surveillance, the end of individual freedoms, and ecological collapse reach their worst and full conclusions in the dystopian novels *Oryx and Crake* (2003), *The Year of the Flood* (2009), and *MaddAddam*

(2013), which is currently being adapted for an HBO television series. These works may recall the "speculative," or as Atwood indicates elsewhere, "blueprint," fiction of *The Handmaid's Tale*, the 1985 Orwellian depiction of a patriarchal, totalitarian theocracy, made into a motion picture film in 1985, and an opera in 2000.

To return to the 1960s, the *Encyclopaedia Britannica* aptly points out how Atwood's early poetry pondered: 1) human behaviour; 2) celebrated the natural world; and 3) condemned materialism. Since *The Circle Game*, winner of the Governor General's Award for Poetry in 1966, we could say that these three objects of contemplation have figured in all of Margaret Atwood's writing since, often with clinical precision and biting wit, and through the use of stunning imagery and symbolism. In the more recent MaddAddam Trilogy, human behaviour extends to the realm of the multicoloured, genetically designed Crakers. The natural world has collapsed under the weight of the worst apocalyptic perils of environmental abuse and capitalist greed presently known to humankind. As for materialism, the recent novel, *The Heart Goes Last*, shows it escalating into a hair-raising confrontation between free will and biopolitical surveillance.

For an appreciation of Margaret Atwood's sharp social pen (or keyboard), her readers can, and do, look, as well to her nonfiction. It is no wonder that she boasts 1.12 million followers on Twitter. Apparently, the Canadian Literature Centre is *not* the only fantastic, forward-looking organization to invite Margaret Atwood to grace its lecture series. *Negotiating with the Dead: A Writer on Writing* (2002) grew out of a series of lectures delivered at the University of Cambridge; *Payback*, the impassioned 2008 CBC Massey Lecture, treats personal and governmental debt as a cultural issue; and with *In Other Worlds: SF and the Human Imagination* (2011), the writer reveals her work's relationship to science fiction. Margaret Atwood does not shy away from current politics either—including hot issues such as prison farms, oil, the G20 Toronto arrests, carbon-reduction treaties, and the social importance of the arts. And then, of course, there was Stephen Harper: the policies, the statements, the hair... Sometimes I wonder if there is a tiny, secret part of Margaret Atwood that misses Stephen Harper and the amount of good material he provided to this political wit and commentator.

Margaret Atwood is a seer, not a moralist. The values of solidarity, forgiveness, and preservation, indeed of precarious lives, run throughout Atwood's storylines. They are what propel her engagement as a writer and as a citizen. Just take the earth's temperature, as Margaret Atwood has been doing these past decades. "Instead of turning life into gold," she urges, "we have the chance to turn gold back into life—good water, fine air, healthy soil, clean energy." Margaret Atwood will not tell us that the world is safe; she tells us to care that *it is not*. She is an ethicist perhaps, showing that to care, and care itself, may indeed not only teach us to survive, but to save ourselves and one another.

MARIE CARRIÈRE
Edmonton, April 2016

The Burgess Shale

In Edmonton, c. 1968–70.

WHEN I WAS LIVING IN EDMONTON from 1968 to 1970, I was old enough to have heard of Henry Kreisel, but too young and inconsequential to actually meet him. He had an extraordinary life and writing career, and I'm happy to be giving, in his honour, this lecture—or reminiscence, or rambling talk, or mixed bag of shards collected from the ruins of time.

When the proposal was first made to me I resisted it. I protested that at my age I was getting beyond the lecture thing, and that my brain was increasingly full of discarded sardine tins, crumpled sheets of waste paper, and empty toothpaste tubes, but the organizers assured me that since they were *my* sardine tins, waste paper, and toothpaste tubes, and since I was iconic and all, and since my work was taught even in high schools, that anything I might bleat forth would be received with polite attention. I hope this will prove to be true. This is not 1970, when things were much rowdier for me. Even though there was not yet any social media in 1970, I used to be called a poetess (which, in that dark antediluvian era when dinosaurs roamed the land, used to mean an inconsequential poet, inconsequential because female) and get complaints about my hair (too long, too curly, too Miltonian, too sinful) and be told that I wrote like a housewife. Fighting words, those.

But now the Granny Effect has set in, and even the rowdiest of younger folk retain some vestigial training from their childhoods, and feel that you should be polite to old folks and not call them poetesses or say rude things about the tops of their heads. It's either politeness or fear. Perhaps the wind of my name guards my ship for a mile around, like Captain Hook's, and they worry that I may blast them into smithereens with one glance from my ironic eyes. Or maybe even my iconic eyes.

I'll mention here that being iconic is not the walk in the park you might suppose. Once upon a time, all you had to do as an iconic fixture was stand around looking wise or possibly made of wood, like real icons. But nowadays you have to smile a lot while people take selfies with you. It's a whole new workout.

Which illustrates one of my points: times change, and as they change, so do the definitions and self-definitions of artists and writers. Who knew what a "selfie" was in 1960? Nobody. The term had not yet been invented.

That being the case, here is the bare-naked truth: I come to you from a planet far, far away and in a distant galaxy, namely the past. "Long past?" Ebenezer Scrooge in Dickens's *A Christmas Carol* asks timorously when told that he is being addressed by the Ghost of Christmas Past. "No," replies the Ghost. "Your past."

And it is of *your* past that I will now discourse. Specifically, your literary past, supposing you are a Canadian; and even more specifically, your literary past of the 1960s—that decade in which the current writing landscape of Canada and the various infrastructures we now take for granted was formed from bits of cosmic alphabetical dust, deformed by the forces of the Great Dark Matter of the eternal Canadian question mark—Do we

And so it goes...

really exist, and if so, as what?—transformed by the grinding action of market forces acting upon intellectual tectonic plates, and squeezed like metamorphic verbal rock into the somewhat peculiar mountains, valleys, lumps, tundras, and swamps we see before us today.

The title of this reconstitutional effort is *The Burgess Shale: The Canadian Writing Landscape of the 1960s*. I will explain my choice of title shortly. But first, I'll begin with the basic question: What do we mean by "writer"?

Every writer answers that question by his or her actual writing: its form, its content, its obsessions, its axioms. And these have something to do with the time in which the writer is writing. What was, or is, the professional infrastructure? Who might publish this "writing?" Who might sell it, who might rip it off without paying (in the early nineteenth century, for instance, there were no copyright laws) and who might collect on it, and how? What are the social assumptions? What is the "role" of the writer that interviewers are so fond of asking about? What is writing "for"—to justify the ways of God to man, to further the triumph of the proletariat, to bear witness to one's times, or simply, if possible, to make a wad of cash? *Who* is writing "for"—the discerning reader, the downtrodden and under-represented, those left alive after a catastrophe, or thrill-seekers looking for romance or a fantasy escape from the mundane? What are the aesthetic assumptions of the writer's era? What is "good" writing, what is "bad" writing? And even: What are the racial and gender and class assumptions taken for granted in the writer's age? Who is supposed to be capable of doing this "writing" of which we speak, and who is not? Why did everyone believe that the author of *Wuthering Heights* was a man? Why did Mary Anne Evans use a pseudonym? Why do some people today believe Shakespeare was really an aristocrat? Today we would knee-jerkingly respond, "In 'writing,' no one's voice should be automatically excluded," but this is a very recent development. Nor are our reactions to writing always as unbiased as we think.

Being of an Aristotelian rather than a Platonic disposition, I'm inclined to say that what writing "is" depends on what is being written at any given time, and how that activity is viewed. "By their fruits ye shall know them," as one famous icon is said to have said, long ago. In 1955 I could have depended on 99 per cent of the Canadian audience to identify that quote—Jesus, for a full ten points—because 99 per cent of the admittedly small number of people likely to read your books in Canada would have had some form of Christian religious education, whether they were Christian or not.

That was due to the peculiar configuration of the Canadian educational system, as determined by the wheeling and dealing that took place at the time of Confederation. The United States separated church and state, but Canada did not. In order to address the interests of overwhelmingly Catholic Québec and also the overwhelmingly Protestant Rest of Canada, there would be a Catholic school board and a Protestant school board, both publicly funded and both expected to incorporate some form of religious instruction within the curriculum. When I tell this to Americans—whose foundational moments include the Declaration of Independence, so thoroughly Enlightenment Eighteenth Century—they make horrified, disbelieving faces, but this was the case. As many have remarked, the geographical

Teen Queen at Niagara Falls, 1954.

space that is now Canada didn't have much of an eighteenth-century Enlightenment, because it was too busy with the French and Indian War. For most of that century New France dominated the territory, with an English Protestant toehold in Nova Scotia, which was then a continuation of New England in the eyes of both itself and its British overlords.

The two-religion public school arrangement was still in full swing when I was attending Grades 1 through 8 in the 1940s, and then Grades 9 through 13 in the 1950s. That's thirteen years of school during which we got prayers and Bible readings every day, memorized psalms and other biblical passages, and took the occasional Religious Knowledge course if some hapless prelate could be lured into giving one, all on the taxpayer's dime. This system collapsed like a slowly melting snowman throughout the 1960s: the publicly funded Catholic schools remained Catholic, but under pressure of religious diversity the publicly funded Protestant schools became secular.

Another seemingly immoveable foundation also evaporated during this period. At the beginning of the 1950s, when Canada was still living in the penumbra of the fading British Empire, the English Literature curriculum was resolutely British. We were taught a Shakespeare play every year. We were fed hefty doses of the English Romantic poets and the Victorians. We managed two Thomas Hardy novels, and *The Mill on the Floss* by George Eliot. We even—in the last year of high school—were allowed some Chaucer, in the original Middle English.

Not any more. The unified curriculum was another thing that crumbled in the 1960s. Thus a present-day writer in Canada—whether in English or in French—can no longer take for granted a shared frame of reference among his or her prospective readers. Which makes teaching—I am told—somewhat more difficult, even at the university level. What can students be expected to know if the subject is any work written before 1960? Where does the title of *Vanity Fair* come from, for a full ten marks? How about *The Sound and the Fury*? *East of Eden*? (Answers: *The Pilgrim's Progress*, by John Bunyan; *Macbeth*, by William Shakespeare; the Book of Genesis, the Bible.) Luckily, help is at hand for the enquiring youthful mind: the internet abounds in study guides that will cough up all sorts of arcane information, some of it actually true, if you have the energy to search. "Seek and ye shall find," as a noteworthy quoter from previous texts once said. Or ye shall find something, though you may be distracted by clickbait invitations to discover what twelve once-famous celebrities look like now. (Who can resist? Not me, evidently, or I wouldn't be telling you this.)

Now, my title: The Burgess Shale.

The Burgess Shale is a very important western Canadian geological formation composed of old, strange fossils. History—in my view—always begins with geology, because geology determines what you can grow and extract, where you can safely build houses without having them demolished by earthquakes, mud slides, and flood plain inundations, which way the water will flow, whether there *is* any water, and what life forms may have flourished in that space before you. We live on a small brown and green skin floating on the surface of our planet, and what it floats on is a sea of rock. Similarly, the present moment may seem self-contained and self-referential, but it too floats on a deeper foundation. Today's poets flower on a subsoil of their dead predecessors. We inherit more than we know.

When asked to write a 250-word overview of my Kreisel Lecture topic, I came up with this, which I quote in part:

The Burgess Shale is a geological formation discovered in the Canadian Rocky Mountains that contains the fossils of many weird and strange early life forms, different from but not unrelated to later and existing forms. I have named my re-visitation of the Canadian writing landscape of the 1960s after it, perhaps whimsically: that period is already fossilized, in a manner of speaking, and it does contain many weird and strange life forms, different from but not unrelated to forms we see today.

How did Canadian writers then see themselves and what they were doing? Did they think of themselves as having "careers," or rather "vocations"? What did they mean by "writer"? What were the elements in their environment that allowed them to flourish, or not? What magazines, physical venues, publishers, bookstores, and attitudes existed then? The generation of the 1960s was instrumental in creating the writer-related institutions and infrastructures we see around us today, from unions and private grant programs and prizes to book tours and book festivals; they did it then, not for fun, but out of perceived need. They were creating spaces for their own writing and that of their peers.

Today's Canadian writing landscape would be mostly unrecognizable to those writing in the 1960s. But just as an arthropod is still an arthropod despite the time that's passed since the Burgess Shale, writing is still writing, and writers are still writers, whatever we mean by that. As with fossils, the prickly bits remain.

The Burgess Shale fossils are noteworthy for the number and oddity of life forms preserved in them, but they are also noteworthy for what they do not contain. They do not contain examples of the life forms that developed after their time: no birds, no mammals, no land-dwelling insects, no primates, no people. Similarly, the Canadian writing scene of the 1960s contains, in retrospect, a number of blank spaces. Things we take for granted today were simply not there.

Let me set the scene for you. Or rather the scenes: the scene in 1960, and then the scene in 1970. I'll talk about what was there and what was not there, and, in some cases, the results attached to each.

In 1960, 50s undergarments were still de rigueur: the steel-plated bra, the impermeable rubber panty girdle that made it appear as if you had a unitary bum. Female hair was to be controlled and shaped—into a helmet or beehive if possible—and kept in place with glue sprayed out of a can. (We still have glue sprayed out of a can, but it is less like liquid Plexiglass, and the spraying method is non-ozone-destroying.) Stockings came in sets of two, since pantyhose had not yet been invented. Many of these stockings still had seams. Birth control pills were unobtainable unless you were married. John F. Kennedy was not elected president of the United States until November 1960; the president at the beginning of 1960 was Dwight Eisenhower. The Civil Rights Movement had not yet exploded in the American South: segregation was still in force. The Vietnam War had not yet been heard of. "Feminism" or "The Women's Movement" was as yet unknown: Betty Friedan's *The Feminine Mystique* was not to appear until 1963.

In culture, broadly interpreted, there were other blanks. Spider-Man, for example, was not launched until 1962. The best-selling novelist in the United States was John O'Hara, with two bestsellers in the same year: *To Kill a Mockingbird* and *Tropic of Cancer* had not yet been published. The Canadian obscenity trial of D.H. Laurence's *Lady Chatterley's Lover* was yet to take place: that would happen in 1962, argued before the Supreme Court by poet-lawyer F.R. Scott, who later wrote a comic poem beginning, "I went to bat for the Lady Chat," and even later was instrumental in forming the League of Canadian Poets.

I recall that event: a small and motley clutch of poets stood on a lawn somewhere in Toronto, having made a declaration of some sort and hammered out a constitution. In those days most poets were male and few had academic jobs, so the group was more proletarian and slightly scruffier—genuinely scruffier—than such a gathering might be today. (If you did have an academic job, it almost certainly did not involve the teaching of "Creative Writing." There were rumours of such things, as there were rumours of Black Masses being performed in graveyards; in the English Departments of the land, such rumours were given equal credence.) The male poets might tell a young female poet—such as myself—that she would never amount to anything unless she fled the university and plunged into the real world, which in their view involved truck-driving.

In 1960, Hugh MacLennan and Morley Callaghan were the big names in Canadian fiction, insofar as there were some. Irving Layton was cutting a swath in poetry, with Leonard Cohen coming on strong. But we were not without international interests: Samuel Beckett's *Waiting For Godot* was widely performed on college campuses and elsewhere. In Canada, the 1960 Governor General's Award for an English-language novel was won by the originally Irish Brian Moore, with *The Luck of Ginger Coffey*. Marie-Claire Blais's *Mad Shadows* had appeared the year before, as had Sheila Watson's *The Double Hook*. Oddly, I studied both of them in an add-on to my fourth-year English Modern Novel course in 1961, of which more later.

In the counter-culture, existentialists, beatniks, folk-singing, and coffee houses that held poetry readings—on less desirable nights, such as Tuesdays—were popular, and black eyeliner was favoured by girls in turtleneck sweaters, for the Juliette Greco look. Cool jazz was hot: Peter Appleyard was its prophet. In pop music, Elvis Presley, the Everly Brothers, Connie Francis, and Chubby Checker were high on the charts. Bob Dylan had not yet appeared, and The Beatles had just formed their band.

Experiments with LSD were underway in such now-unlikely places as the University of Western Ontario, but neither acid nor marijuana had yet gone mainstream. A woman wearing a pantsuit could not go into a cocktail lounge. In fact, there were no women wearing pantsuits. There were no pantsuits.

Jump to 1970. Having been through the assassination of Kennedy, the Civil Rights Movement, the advent of the widely-distributed Pill and thus the "sexual revolution" during which marriages exploded like popcorn, the arrival of thousands of American draft dodgers from the Vietnam War, the deployment of pot and acid throughout youth culture and beyond, the mini-skirt and Twiggy, the Summer of Love and hippies, and the first blast of the Women's Movement, we arrived at the 1970s sporting the "ethnic look"—curly hair was in, at last—and, yes, pantsuits. Many changes had taken place in the culture at large; and, in the smaller world of Canadian writing and publishing, many changes had also taken place.

Here is a list of what, at the beginning of the decade in question, in the Canadian book world, there was not. There was no email: we sent our manuscripts in quaint paper structures called "envelopes," with a self-addressed, stamped return envelope enclosed; if you did not include the return envelope you would never get your manuscript back, with the typed

Poetry night, Bohemian Embassy, Toronto, 1960. Sylvia Tyson on guitar.

rejection letter attached. There were no book tours as such: these were to arrive later in the decade, the brainchild of Jack McClelland of McClelland and Stewart. There were no literary festivals: they began in the 1970s. The first free-standing writers' festival I know of was the International Harbourfront Festival in Toronto, a spin-off from the coffee-house culture of the early 60s. There were no electric typewriters. And of course there was no internet, so there were no online book purchasing sites or book bloggers or social media campaigns. There were also no literary agents as such in Canada. For that reason, most Canadian writers—with the exception of older ones such as Morley Callaghan, who'd published in other countries—had scant knowledge of the business side of writing: what should be covered by a contract, what they might expect as an advance, and so forth. There were few genre writers—little crime, or sci-fi. There was, as yet, not much publishing for children, apart from Sunday school magazines. There was no "YA" category. There were no Canadian comic book artists who lived in Canada, although there were political cartoonists—those had a long and venerable tradition. In the wartime 40s there had been some homegrown black-and-whites—*Johnny Canuck*, *Nelvana of the North*—but by 1960 they were long forgotten.

In the other arts, there was no Canadian film industry at the beginning of the 60s, apart from the short films and documentaries made largely by the NFB. There was hardly any professional theatre, the touring companies that used to visit Canada having been knocked out by the war. The Canadian Opera Company had just been formed. The Royal Winnipeg Ballet already existed, as did the National Ballet, just barely. The Stratford Festival was in its toddler years. There were a couple of symphony orchestras. There was jazz, here and there. There was

CBC Radio, arguably more vigorous and eccentric than it has since become. Television was in its early stages. Most television watched at that time was American network television, and it was black and white. There was no cable.

The visual arts were more vigorous. There were some adventurous private galleries in the larger cities. Did I actually attend an exhibit of a show by Mark Prent that was set up like a butcher's shop, only with human body parts in the white enamel trays, including a tray of penises? I did. It was at the Av Isaacs Gallery. The police closed it down.

There were a couple of literary prizes, though the Governor General's Awards were the only big ones, and "big" was an extremely relative term. When I won this prize myself, in 1967, the sum was $1,000, which—granted—went farther then, but was still not exactly enormous.

Not that I wasn't thrilled with it. I bought an electric typewriter, the very latest model. (It was not yet a Selectric, which—Wow!—allowed you to type italics by changing a sort of metal type ball above the keyboard.) I also bought some contact lenses. These were still the hard kind—the Model T of contact lenses—so I spent the next ten years screaming, clapping my hand to my eye, then groping around in the mashed potatoes for a fallen lens. When I needed to alter a manuscript—done, in those days, with a small bottle of Wite-Out and a little brush—I would take the contact lenses out, all the better to see my typos with. (The advent of the personal computer put an end to the little white bottle, much to the dismay of literary scholars, who like to follow meandering trails of manuscript corrections as if writers were snails.)

At the beginning of the decade—in 1960—there was only a handful of publishers in English Canada who published books

First "real" book published (Contact Press, 1966).
Cover: Letraset + Legal Dots.

by Canadians. Of these, most were "branch plants"—their head offices were elsewhere, in cultural capitals such as London, New York, and Paris (for francophones). Oxford University Press and Macmillan were among these branch plants. Some publishers, such as The Ryerson Press and McClelland and Stewart and the notoriously teetotalling Clarke Irwin, which served grape juice at book launches, were Canadian-owned.

But in order to publish anything so substantial as a novel with one of the bigger publishers, you needed to have a book they thought they might be able to sell, and since they considered the Canadian reading public to be both small and provincial, that usually meant co-publication with a British or American or French publisher. At that time—when Canada was viewed as uninteresting, both to the bigger countries and to its own readers—this wasn't easy.

In 1960 there were five novels by Canadian writers published in English Canada by Canadian publishers. That's the fingers of one hand, for the whole year. By the end of the decade this situation had changed considerably, and it was to change even more in the 1970s. Part of what happened in the decade was the growth of a Canadian audience for Canadian books. (Perhaps we should say the "re-growth," as such an audience had existed, once, before the war.) A parallel development was the appearance of a number of smaller publishers. Each fuelled the other.

In 1960 there were a few literary magazines of varying sizes and professionalism, though each one of them, however thin and mimeographed, was important to youthful would-be literati such as myself. There were a couple of small presses that specialized in poetry, and they were frequently—like Contact Press and Delta—run by poets. On the other hand, there were more glossy magazines then that would publish fiction—*Chatelaine* did—and some that are now defunct, such as *Montreal Magazine*. Some of the newspapers would publish fiction as well, usually in their weekend supplements—weekend supplements still existed.

There were no grants from the Canada Council for the Arts or from anyone else that enabled writers to travel and give readings and meet other writers, or to complete works in progress. As I've said, there were no creative writing programmes in universities, with the exception of the one that had just been started at the University of British Columbia by Earle Birney and Warren Tallman over the dead bodies of various English Literature professors. And there were certainly no creative writing programmes in high schools. You were taught to write essays, with half a point off for spelling mistakes. "My Summer Holidays" was about as creative as it got.

I know this is sounding a lot like "We were so poor I had a sock for a pet" and "You young folks don't know how good you've got it," but so it was. On the positive side, there's nothing so motivating as a blank page. It cries out to be scribbled on. It fosters improvisation and invention, and the Canadian writers of the 1960s did a lot of improvising and inventing, because they had to.

To add a little flavour from those times—improvisational, inventive, and far from top-heavy with a sense of their own importance—I'll describe two peculiar moments, not from the 1960s, but from the 1970s. Neither one of these moments would have been possible in the 1950s, and both would have been unlikely in the 1980s. It is probable that neither is recorded in any official history of Canadian literature or publishing. Those moments are The All-Star Eclectic Typewriter Revue and the Writers' Union of Canada's failed pornography project.

The poster for The All-Star Eclectic Typewriter Revue.

The first, the All-Star Eclectic Typewriter Revue, took place possibly in 1974. Or maybe 1975. Or it could even have been 1976. A poster for it exists—it is hanging on one of my walls. (For the very youthful: posters, in that age before the internet, were one of the ways we got the word out about events. We used to sneak around at night and staple them up on hoardings, and place them in bookstores. Where are the posters of yesteryear? On the internet, if anywhere.) The month and the date are on this poster, but not the year, so I don't know exactly which year it was.

The Revue was a fundraising evening put on by the assembled prose writers of English Canada in aid of the Writers' Union, which had just been formed in 1973, again with the help of F.R. Scott and his constitution-writing skills. One reason it was formed was the absence of literary agents. Writers had no one to represent their interests—the interests of writers, as opposed to those of publishers, readers, and libraries. The three latter felt in their hearts that simply being read was honour enough for a writer: no money need be forthcoming. The writers, on the other hand, took the quaint and possibly dangerously Communist position that what they did was work, and they ought to be remunerated by those making use of that work.

Plus ça change. Those holding the view that writers' work is like air, to be had for the breathing, now include assorted internet pundits and a great many universities, those bastions of freedom of speech and fair dealing. But I digress.

The Writers' Union itself was an aftermath of the Ontario Royal Commission on Book Publishing, held in 1972. And the Commission was a response to the sale of The Ryerson Press—a venerable institution, and one of the few Canadian-owned publishers—to the US firm of McGraw-Hill in 1970, which caused an outcry in the writing and publishing communities. Several young writers, Graeme Gibson among them, scaled the statue of Edgerton Ryerson in Toronto and draped it in an American flag. This caper—and the attendant poster, stapled upon hoardings—made the newspapers. Writing and publishing had come to seem very important to the country's image of itself: it was deemed crucial to have a homegrown publishing industry that would publish books by Canadians and about Canada.

That wasn't self-evident in 1959, but by 1969 it was an accepted attitude. The generation of 60s writers had helped to create that attitude, for better or for worse. For worse? Yes, there is always a worse. No rule makes it so that just because a book is by a Canadian and published in Canada, it is therefore well written and engrossing. But never mind: every country produces work that is ultimately not of much interest, so why should Canada be an exception?

Thus, in the mid-70s, there was the infant Writers' Union, and, as always, it was in pursuit of cash to keep itself going. The All-Star Eclectic Typewriter Revue—for the very young, the title is a pun on "electric typewriter," that snazzy and coveted innovation of that time—the Revue was one of the Union's money-raising efforts, and a great success it was. It packed St. Lawrence Hall, for one night only. Onstage was a range of acts, from Rudy Wiebe and Andreas Schroeder singing beautiful Mennonite duets, to Pierre Berton reciting his party piece, Robert Service's " The Shooting of Dan McGrew," to Jack McClelland, The Canadian Publisher, wandering onstage in a vampire cloak and wax fangs while Hélène Holden sang a spirited rendition of "Jack the Knife." (For the very young, this is a pun on "Mack the Knife," from *The Threepenny Opera*.)

I myself headed up the Farley Mowat Dancers, a group of six short women who, when outfitted in fur coats, tuques, beards, and snowshoes for our first number, "Lost in the Barrens," looked remarkably like six short, bearded, fur-coated Farley Mowats. The snowshoes were quite dangerous on the hardwood stage; I almost killed us. I forget what the second Farley Mowat Dancer number was called, but it involved kilts.

My *chef-d'oeuvre* as an impresario, however, was a piece called The Toronto Literary Mafia, which was then a generally-understood term denoting the literary critics of the three main book-review players of Canada, those of the *Globe and Mail*, the *Toronto Star*, and *Saturday Night* magazine. I talked the three dignified and skittish literary critics of the day into performing in the piece by telling them the other two had agreed to do it, a standard director's trick. Then I had to get them to wear black shirts, white ties, fedoras, and—for Robert Fulford, playing the Godfulford—a black homburg. I also had to teach them to dance the cha-cha, for the chorus—sung offstage by an opera singer to the tune of the Chiquita Banana commercial, since the three of them wisely balked at actually singing. This number was a tremendous hit, especially since one of the literary critics couldn't dance. Bill French of the *Globe* was quite agile and dapper, Douglas Marshall of the *Star* was lumpy though competent, but Robert Fulford just kind of swayed back and forth. During rehearsals—or rather "rehearsal," since there was only one—he despaired. " They'll love it," I said encouragingly, which proved to be true. Fulford brought down the house, and got an A for Best Effort.

Here I will pause to comment that Canada is, or was then, a skit-making nation, and Canadians will make fun of almost anything. Also, if you refuse to make fun of yourself, the hot-air balloon that is your swelled head will be swiftly punctured by your fellow Canadians. They do it as a kindness—modesty is considered a virtue, and if you don't have enough of it the civic-minded will help you out. This trait can be confusing to, for instance, Europeans of the old school, for whom authorship should be august and somewhat furrowing to the brow, and it can also be daunting for young artists, who need a certain amount of *amour propre* just to keep themselves going. But so it is. For those who doubt me, I cite Alice Munro's *Lives of Girls and Women*, in which young Del Jordan's worst fear is that people will find out about her artistic ambitions and then laugh at her.

So the All-Star Eclectic Typewriter Revue fit right into a long-standing Canadian tradition, and was, as we say, well received. That was one of our fundraising efforts. The second one—the pornography project—came to nothing in and of itself. Whose idea was it? Who knows? The concept was that—following the lead of *Naked Came the Stranger*—we would write a collective pornographic opus and sell it for a lot of money. For the moderately young, *Naked Came the Stranger* was a 1969 literary hoax written by twenty-four US journalists. They set out to create a deliberately awful book with a lot of sex in it as a way of exposing the bad taste and vulgarity of the times, and they did in fact produce a bestseller, thus proving their point. (I should add that this was in an age still relatively porn-free: the internet had not yet unleashed the present deluge of contorted flesh upon the world. Risqué prose was still risky business, *Playboy* centerfolds were relatively demure, and the real stuff, such as it was, went on under the counter. Not that it would raise much of an eyebrow today, going in as it did for garter belts and black D-cup brassieres.)

Why should we Canadian literary writers not produce our own *Naked Came the Stranger* as a fundraiser, we wondered? As it turned out, there was a very good reason: as writers of erotica we were terrible. The majority of those who took the pledge never delivered. Of those who did, most ended up writing parodies. One of our number began in earnest—she was writing an erotic piece about a woman having a love affair with a bear—very Canadian, and at least it wasn't a moose or a beaver—but she became fascinated with the implications, and her porn piece turned into a literary novel of high quality called *Bear*. The author was Marian Engel, and she scooped the Governor General's Award for 1976. Yes, a Governor General's Award winner began as a money-raising hunk o' porn! From such peculiar acorns do mighty oak trees grow. I'm happy to report that *Bear* has recently had a revival due to its trashy paperback cover. Such is often the effect of trashy paperback covers.

My own porn-project attempt turned very quickly into a literary parody; in fact, five literary parodies. It was called "Regional Romances; or, Across Canada by Pornograph"—as you can see, the great Canadian motif of trans-continental communication was already being incorporated into it. It dealt with five regions—the Maritimes, Québec, Ontario, the Prairies, and British Columbia. Each episode was written in a style and with themes appropriate to the fiction of its region. It also made deft use of the asterisk, a much-underrated punctuation mark.

The fourth section—the Prairie one—was titled, "As For Me and My Grain Elevator; or, Over Prairie Trulls." You will recognize this title immediately as a reference to Sinclair Ross's wonderful Prairie Depression classic, *As For Me and My House*, featuring the never-first-named Mrs. Bentley and her marital troubles with her husband, a minister, combined with another Prairie classic, *Over Prairie Trails*, by Frederick Philip Grove. Or maybe you won't recognize it. (The hero of my piece is named

Spot. For those not brought up on the *Dick and Jane* primary school readers, Spot was their dog.)

From "Regional Romances," here is:

AS FOR ME AND MY GRAIN ELEVATOR;
Or, Over Prairie Trulls.

Mrs. Warped was sitting at her flat, cheap, meagre, narrow, worn, mean-minded, provincial kitchen table. It was covered with grey linoleum. Once, the linoleum had been a gay, lively shade of grey, sprigged with grey flowers; but the years had worn it down so that it was now grey. Mrs. Warped sighed. The years had worn her down too, years of snow, dust, hail, and rust and the evil-minded gossip of the nasty, shrunken inhabitants of the constricted little town of Sphincter, Sask. She looked into the yellowing, cracked, dwarfish mirror over the grey kitchen sink and sighed again. She was grey. She had once been a fairly pretty woman but now she looked old, old and frowsy, with fallen arches and tired blood. And she was only twelve. No wonder her husband, Spot, hardly touched her any more. . . .

Spot was an orphan, named by one of the nurses at the institution for a character in the only book she'd ever read. It was hard being a minister—especially in a narrow-minded place like Sphincter—saddled with a name like Spot. Sphincter was so culturally deprived, she thought. She had once played the washboard in a skiffle band, but there was no outlet for that kind of thing here.

As she sat at the kitchen table trying to remember her first name, she heard Spot's study door slam. He was always slamming his study door, even though she'd asked him not to. He did it so often she suspected it of being some kind of sexual perversion. She'd often wondered how he was getting it off; it certainly wasn't with her. It was grating on her nerves. If he did it once more she was tempted to kick him in the balls.

She tiptoed to the study with his evening glass of hot milk and peeped in. Spot wasn't there! But the window was open, and through it she could see the endless flat prairie, which was grey in colour.

So that was it! Slamming the study door was a ruse, so he could sneak out and prowl around at night, in search of freedom. Not that she didn't understand. . .she too wanted her freedom. Many times she had longed to run along the railroad tracks, flinging off her wedgies and white ankle socks. . .but you couldn't do things like that in Sphincter.

Mrs. Warped slipped through the open window. She was just in time to see Spot entering the barn, with a lantern. He must be meeting someone there, she thought. Their one cow had already been fed, so that wasn't the explanation. She would confront him, she would find out the truth. . . .

As she peered around the corner of the barn door, an astonishing sight met her eyes. Spot was standing in front of the cow—which looked bored and skeptical—in a suggestive pose, one hand on his chest, the other outflung in a gesture of abandonment. As she watched, an expression of obscene pleasure transformed his face. This was not the Spot she knew!

"Ontario stinks!" he said, in a seductive and forceful voice.

"So!" she said, stepping out to confront him. "This is how you've been spending your evenings!"

Spot was surprised to see her, but not dismayed. "It's not what you think," he said. "I'm just practicing."

"Practicing what?" she demanded. If he was going to be unfaithful, at least he could admit it like a man.

"I'm leaving the ministry," he said. "Sphincter is too small to hold me. I'm going into provincial politics."

Mrs. Warped sighed with relief. Everything was explained.

The Ontario entry was called "ROUGHING IT IN THE BUSHES: The Real Journals of Suzanna Floozie." The Québec one was called "LA PLUME DE MA TANT PIS; Or, Growing Up Before The Revolution, When Times Were Worse but Writing About Them Was More Fun." It was suitably surrealistic. The British Columbia entry—which lacked capital letters in that age of late hippiedom and bill bissett—was called "ON TOP OF MOUNT SEYMOUR, a beecee novul."

Every entry except the one from Québec contained a very filthy but titillating phrase, which was revealed, in each case, at the end. That phrase was—dare I pronounce it in polite company?—that phrase was, "Ontario stinks." Ah, nostalgia—once upon a time, Ontario was universally reviled for being rich and dominant. Then it was Alberta's turn to be universally reviled, for the same reasons. But who knows what the reality is any more?

"Regional Romances: Across Canada by Pornograph" has never been published, but for a suitable sum I might consider... No! What am I saying? I am a serious writer and an icon, and icons are not supposed to do that sort of thing.

Point being that neither of these wrinkles in time—the Revue and the porn project—would have been possible at any other moment. The porn project, although it failed, was a noble exercise in self-sacrifice in aid of the general good. The Revue brought together Canadian writers from all age groups, and from across the country, working as a team and making idiots of themselves for a common cause.

Would you be able to field such an event now? Probably not. Canadian literary culture has become too vast, too diverse, and too classified into "genres"; it would be hard to cram it all under one roof, or even to make jokes about that everyone—or everyone likely to pay any attention—would understand. As for the porn project, no one today would even think of it. Porn is so widespread it's no longer of much interest as a subject either for serious exploration or for parody. It's just there—a condition of our modern life, like fast food. It's not good for you; many suffer in its production; but it's highly lucrative.

The outburst of cultural energy that took place in the 1960s was in part a product of the two decades that came before. It's always difficult for young people to see their own time in perspective: when you're in your teens, a decade earlier feels like ancient history and the present moment seems normal: what exists now is surely what has always existed. But as the years pass by, you realize this isn't true: your own first decades are just as much of a snapshot in time as other decades were.

What came before the 60s were the 50s, and what came before the 50s were the 40s; and in the 40s was World War II, which in retrospect marked a huge rift in the cultural life of Canada.

Before the war, Canadians thought of themselves as a junior part of the British Empire. So did they during the war, and for perhaps ten years after its end. But by the mid-60s, they didn't so much. Hardly at all. The Empire itself had largely crumbled, and the new Empire—the American one—was in the ascendant.

When writing a novel, I find it helpful to make a chart that has the months of the year down the left-hand side and the years across the top. I can then place the birth dates of the characters exactly, and I will always know how old these people are, in relation not only to the other characters, but also to the world events and the national and even local ones that are taking place.

I will now do that for myself. I was born in 1939; I was thus of an age to remember the end of the war, though not its beginning. The pop-cultural forms of the 1940s were the movies—many and varied—and radio—including radio drama, comedy shows, and soap operas. Television was in its infancy. There were also the funny papers, with their joined-at-the-hip multi-platform, the comic book. Everyone read the funny papers: boys, girls, men, women. Comics had not yet become the nerdy enclave they are seen as being today.

In the late 1940s there was still a mood of postwar optimism and euphoria. Consumer goods, so scarce during the war, began to spew forth in profusion. As rationing ended, a huge amount of meat was consumed, and orange juice flowed like wine. (It was hard to get oranges during the war.) After two decades of austerity, the economy was growing and people were in the mood to spend. Automobiles, vacuum cleaners, and washing machines made a fortune. Technicolor cameras broke out like measles, which also broke out—there was not yet a measles vaccine. The ranch bungalow, the four-child family, and the dream that was shortly to be exploded by housewifely rebellion was underway, though it was preceded by house-husbandly rebellion in the form of *Playboy* magazine, launched by Hugh Hefner in 1953 to capitalize on the ennui suffered by men in grey flannel suits, back from the war, stuffed into civilian jobs, and bored by the sedateness of the lives they were now expected to lead. For an overview and an analysis of the social flavour of the late 1940s and early 1950s, nothing beats Marshall McLuhan's first book, the wise-cracking, smart-talking *The Mechanical Bride: Folklore of Industrial Man* (1951), which made its points by deconstructing popular advertisements of the day.

In 1960 you couldn't buy this book in a bookstore because some of the companies whose ads had been deconstructed in it objected, and invoked copyright law. But you could buy it on the sly from the stash in Marshall McLuhan's cellar, which we students did.

The arts in Canada had been dealt a blow by the Depression, and another one by the war: you can see how that might have been. Creative energy and money had to go into the war, and they did. Nascent writing careers had been nipped in the bud: for instance, *As For Me And My House*, by Sinclair Ross—the model for "As For Me and My Grain Elevator"—was unlucky enough to be published in 1939, at the war's outbreak, and it sank like a stone, only to be revived later via Jack McClelland's heroic archaeological project, the New Canadian Library. (Too late for Sinclair Ross, however, whose published correspondence with Jack McClelland and others is called *Collecting Stamps Would Have Been More Fun.*)

I should explain here that the advent of the paperback book played a key role in the way in which Canadian writing and publishing developed in the 1960s. The modern paperback took shape in the 1930s, via Penguin—a well-written book for the price of a package of cigarettes was its model, a wildly successful one—and then took the USA by storm in the 1940s, under Pocket Books. Pocket Books and its imitators published quality books with trashy covers that were distributed, typically, in drug stores rather than book stores. You could buy genuinely trashy books there, such as Mickey Spillane's Mike Hammer detective stories. Or you could buy classics by Hemingway, Faulkner, or Orwell with trashy covers on them—I expect a lot of kids were lured into good reading that way. But in either case, such books were very unlikely to be Canadian, because the paperback houses were owned in the United States.

The paperback industry wiped out the vestiges of the old Canadian publishing system that had flourished before the war by selling cheap hardback editions. In the 50s, a book would be published in hardback, but then, after its run, it would simply vanish. The result for us young writers was that we had little access to Canadian writing of earlier years unless we already knew about it and could search it out in libraries. We therefore felt artistically rootless, at least in relation to Canada. The writers and books we admired were likely to come from elsewhere.

Thus we young writers in 1960 thought—and indeed were told by older writers, should we be lucky enough to encounter any—that if we wanted to amount to anything we would have to leave Canada for larger places where there was actually some culture, such as New York or London. Many writers a decade older than us had done just that: Mordecai Richler, Mavis Gallant, and Margaret Laurence were all living abroad at this time—not that any of us had heard of them as yet.

In 1960, when I was twenty, I thought that there hadn't been any modern Canadian writing, much—we weren't taught it as a subject in school, though the odd Canadian snippet for older times made its way in, amongst Thomas Hardy and Shakespeare and George Eliot. An Archibald Lampman sonnet, a Pauline Johnson standby. However, once I was seen as a young poet, I met some other poets, and became aware of the A.J.M. Smith anthology, and the *Oxford Book of Canadian Verse*. That was something. And Robert Weaver's radio programme, *Anthology*, was known to every young writer: he actually paid! How radical! His first volume of Canadian short stories appeared around that time.

There was also a whole vanished history from a period less than twenty years before of which we knew nothing. Gwethalyn Graham wrote a huge bestseller—the 1944 *Earth and High Heaven*—featuring a romance between a Jewish man and a non-Jewish woman: tricky business and very political at that time. It topped the *New York Times* chart for many months. And Gabrielle Roy published an even bigger seller, *Bonheur d'Occasion*—translated as *The Tin Flute*—in 1946. Its 1947 American print run was a staggering 700,000 copies. (This was in an age when the Literary Guild had a huge influence on book sales, and *The Tin Flute* was a Guild pick.) I did know about Gabrielle Roy; one of her books was a set text for the Grade 13 French exam in 1957. But it was a later, less controversial book: *La Petite Poule d'Eau*, a far less racy affair.

The reason this book was chosen, rather than the earlier, more incendiary Montreal-slum one, was probably the change that took place in the social climate at the beginning of the 1950s. McCarthyism had set in, with its Red Scares and trials. The Cold War was underway, the atomic bomb was the incarnation of a possible Armageddon, and anything having to do with what we would now call "social justice" sounded like Communism. Catchwords that had been common and even expected in the 1930s and the 1940s were now out. You couldn't draw attention to horrible slum conditions, or say "working class" or even "world peace" any more without being suspected of being a Commie stooge.

Our generation of college students—entering in the late 50s, graduating in the early 60s—was told by our professors that we were quite tame and listless compared with the 30s radicals and the late-40s returning vets that had preceded us. We were conformists; we weren't bent on expanding our minds, just in becoming well-paid professionals. Those of us who were interested in the arts were few, and were viewed as affected and strange by the bulk of the student body. If you thought you might actually devote your life to such things, you were seen as delusional. In 1961 I was told by my faculty advisor that I should forget about writing and going to graduate school; instead, I should find a good man and get married. Luckily I had other faculty advisors with other views. I was also pig-headed, which can get you through a lot if you are really determined.

Was Canada a cultural wasteland in 1960? Not exactly. I'd call it a locus of robust amateurism and do-it-yourselfery. If you fooled around in the arts, you frequently found yourself multitasking: acting one moment, painting sets the next, doing magazine layout, then writing the material to put into the magazine under several different names. These qualities came in handy when it was time for a bunch of kids who really didn't know what they were doing to start new publishing companies in Canada, which we did in the 1960s. And due to demographics—low birth rates in the 30s, courtesy the Depression and also during the war, followed by the baby boom—those born in the middle 1930s to the middle 1940s found that their services—whatever they were—were much in demand. You didn't worry then about not being able to get a job; you simply worried about which job.

Our generation inherited a relative cultural emptiness. We sought to fill it. We made cultural artefacts out of the materials at hand. If we had lived in an older, more recognized, more celebrated cultural milieu, we might have been intimidated. We might not have tried. As it was, we ventured. We didn't see why not.

The 1960s was a time when poetry had an importance in the literary landscape that it hasn't had since—partly because it was so hard to get novels published. Reading poetry aloud—starting with the beats and City Lights Bookstore in San Francisco—had become the coffee-house movement; that's where the likes of me got our start.

Among the young writers I knew, most were poets. We gathered our poems into collections, of which we didn't expect to sell more than a couple of hundred copies. Some of us had prose ambitions, but none thought they could make a living on their writing alone, on the Morley Callaghan model: go to the States, write stories for the glossy magazines. Such a career path might have been possible in the 20s or even in the 30s, but it now seemed out of our reach.

We didn't think of ourselves as professionals in that way. The kind of writing we wanted to do was experimental, quirky, non-commercial.

We had very scant notions about the market or how to sell things, or any of that. We didn't think of writing as a career, but as a vocation—a calling. Sheila Watson and Marie-Claire Blais were the kind of writers we had in mind—non-traditional novelists, both of them. In my case, it helped that both were female.

I came across them in 1961. I was twenty-one; it was my fourth and final year at Victoria College, University of Toronto.

I was in a course called English Language and Literature, which took the student from Anglo-Saxon to T.S. Eliot, covering everything in between. At the very end, as a sort of dessert, we were allowed a course in the Modern Novel, and at the very end of that, as a sort of double espresso, we were given two books by Canadians: *The Double Hook*, by Sheila Watson, and *Mad Shadows*, which was the English translation title of *La Belle Bête*, by Marie-Claire Blais.

We didn't study Canadian literature as such in Eng Lang and Lit, so these books weren't on the course because they were specifically Canadian. I think they were chosen because of their unconventional forms. In the case of *The Double Hook*, with its terse intercut short sequences, you might say "modernist." *Mad Shadows* was a supercharged anti-fairy tale of jealousy, narcissism, and revenge, written by a nineteen-year-old and praised by Edmund Wilson. It was a formidable role model for a similarly-aged young female writer such as myself.

Not incidentally, both of these books appeared in soft covers, but with elegant rather than trashy designs. They were what we would now call "trade paperbacks," though that term did not yet exist. The format made a statement: these books are experimental, so we, the publishers, cannot take the chance of placing them in expensive hardback editions.

I was very impressed by these covers. They were like the Grove Press editions from the United States I was also reading at the time. They were like Samuel Beckett. They were the equivalent of black eyeliner. I wanted some. This was probably the height of my ambition in 1961: to exist between covers like that. I thought I would be obscure, known only to other poets. That was the general fate of poets at the time, except for Leonard Cohen.

But there's an advantage to being small and obscure. If you aren't wedded to the market, and to the expectation of making

With Al Purdy and Avi Boxer at a Montreal party, 1968.

it big, and to the anxieties of your publisher, you are in fact freer to create whatever strikes your fancy; and so it was in the early 60s. One of the stranger manifestations of that period was James Reaney's hand-set magazine, *Alphabet*. And Reaney himself among the quirkier Canadian talents—his long poem, *A Suit of Nettles*, is a series of Spenserian eclogues delivered by the members of a flock of geese. When you come to think of it, this is remarkably odd.

The decade abounds with similar oddities—Larry Garber's story "Death by Toilet," Joe Rosenblatt's Egg poems, the sound poetry of bill bissett and also that of the Four Horsemen. None of this was aimed at the general reading public, though the general reading public shortly became interested in it—for, in the mid-60s, the newspapers noticed the fact that these bizarre things were happening, and began to write about them. Even Members of Parliament noticed, and denounced poets from the floor of the House. Those were the days!

The years 1966–67 were possibly a hinge moment—the moment when smallness and obscurity turned the corner into a more public phase. First, a new cultural nationalism arose, fuelled by the hosting by Canada of Expo '67, the international exposition that took place in Montreal that year and was a great success. Concurrently, the young writers were founding publishing companies—Coach House Press and the House of Anansi Press both appeared around that time. Both first specialized in poetry, and both saw themselves as outlets for experimental writing that were not being provided by the more traditional publishers. Anansi was co-founded by Dennis Lee, a classmate at university, so I was soon drawn—I will not say "sucked"—into its orbit. One of the things we tried to do was keep prices down, so my earlier book-cover ambition—soft covers, but elegant design—was realized.

These were also the years when Jack McClelland of McClelland and Stewart—then a Canadian-owned publishing house—was throwing his weight behind Canadian writing. That was, again, a function of changes in publishing economics—high schools were scrapping the set curriculum, thus jerking the rug out from under the publishers that had depended on a steady and dependable market of *Julius Caesars* and *Mills on the Floss*—and Jack saw an opening, and went for it. He would be "the Canadian publisher," a distinction nobody else—yet—seemed to want.

"I don't publish books, I publish authors," he said to me at the moment when he took me on as a fiction writer. It was 1967. I was wearing a Mao jacket with brass buttons, with a mini-skirt, and maybe it was the jacket that convinced him I was a viable literary commodity.

To support his Canadian authors, Jack invented the cross-Canada book tour. (In those days there were no phoners or email interviews: you had to go to a city to get any press there.) Jack did book tours before US publishing took them up—and he became well known for being willing to do anything to sell a book. It was he who, to promote a book on snakes, sent out a number of boxes with breathing holes in them to all the book reviewers, triggering a rash of screaming and frantic calls to the humane society by editors who thought the snakes must have got out. To publicize a book on football, it was miniature jock straps. It should be said that Jack and many of the writers of his own age that he so adored, such as Farley Mowat, were veterans of World War II, and similarly devil-may-care. We kids must have seemed pretty boring to them.

Above: First jacket photo. Picture by artist Charles Pachter.

Left: First novel published, 1969. Cover by Charles Pachter.

What did we think we were doing, we young writers of that decade? Who did we think we were?

It was a time of considerable turmoil, but also one of euphoria—we really believed we were opening up new subjects and experimenting with new forms, and, yes, describing Canadian landscapes and cityscapes in a way that hadn't been done before. And we were doing that, up to a point.

As we moved into the 70s, large new possibilities were forming around us. An audience had been created, and Canadian writing was suddenly a viable commercial proposition. Branch plants took it seriously. The Canada Council for the Arts was now in operation, and grants multiplied. Creative writing programmes began in earnest. Literary festivals sprang up. Prizes proliferated. Eventually, genre writers appeared, beginning with crime writers. We hadn't had those before.

"CanLit" became a term. Arguments broke out over it. Insults were exchanged. Did we finally have a cultural identity? "Canada comes of age" was a slogan we'd heard a little too often, but maybe this was the real thing. At least it was a conversation.

Jump a few decades, to 2016.

Right now we're in yet another age of turmoil, with different sorts of possibilities having been created by the internet: self-publishing, online magazines, blogs, and so forth. The cards, once again, are in the air. People shake their heads over the future of reading, while at the same time words pour forth in ever-increasing numbers from ever-increasing numbers of authors.

Never has so much been written by so many for the benefit—we are told—of so few readers. The math does not compute: maybe the bean counters are counting the wrong beans? But the traditional book is not dead, despite the assurance of a few years ago that it would be entirely replaced by the e-book. Strangely, the paper dinosaur seems to have a good deal of life in it yet.

I won't risk any predictions about the future of reading, of writing, or of publishing, or even of storytelling. Frankly, I think the narrative and poetic impulses can look after themselves just fine, assuming there's still a livable planet to house them. Exactly how the future will unfold won't be up to me, however: it will be up to you.

If you're twenty, you are the age I was in 1960. You're entering your experimental decade. Make new life forms! Create new fossils for future generations to unearth! Plunge in!

CLC Kreisel Lecture Series

From Mushkegowuk to New Orleans
A Mixed Blood Highway
JOSEPH BOYDEN
ISBN 978–1–897126–29–5

The Old Lost Land of Newfoundland
Family, Memory, Fiction, and Myth
WAYNE JOHNSTON
ISBN 978–1–897126–35–6

Un art de vivre par temps de catastrophe
DANY LAFERRIÉRE
ISBN 978–0–88864–553–1

The Sasquatch at Home
Traditional Protocols & Modern Storytelling
EDEN ROBINSON
ISBN 978–0–88864–559–3

Imagining Ancient Women
ANNABEL LYON
ISBN 978–0–88864–629–3

Dear Sir, I Intend to Burn Your Book
An Anatomy of a Book Burning
LAWRENCE HILL
ISBN 978–0–88864–679–8

Dreaming of Elsewhere
Observations on Home
ESI EDUGYAN
ISBN 978–0–88864–821–1

A Tale of Monstrous Extravagance
Imagining Multilingualism
TOMSON HIGHWAY
ISBN 978–1–77212–041–7

Who Needs Books?
Reading in the Digital Age
LYNN COADY
ISBN 978–1–77212–124–7

The Burgess Shale
The Canadian Writing Landscape of the 1960s
MARGARET ATWOOD
ISBN 978–1–77212–301–2

My Education
On unusual muses and mentors. And how I had to teach myself everything in order to cross the class divide.
HEATHER O'NEILL
coming 2018